KENDRICK LAMAR

KENDRICK LAMAR

Platinum Rap Artist

HEATHER E. SCHWARTZ

LERNER PUBLICATIONS ◆ MINNEAPOLIS

Copyright © 2024 by Lerner Publishing Group, Inc.

All rights reserved. International copyright secured. No part of this book may be reproduced, stored in a retrieval system, or transmitted in any form or by any means—electronic, mechanical, photocopying, recording, or otherwise—without the prior written permission of Lerner Publishing Group, Inc., except for the inclusion of brief quotations in an acknowledged review.

Lerner Publications Company
An imprint of Lerner Publishing Group, Inc.
241 First Avenue North
Minneapolis, MN 55401 USA

For reading levels and more information, look up this title at www.lernerbooks.com.

Main body text set in Rotis Serif Std 55 Regular. Typeface provided by Adobe Systems.

Editor: Karen Latchana Kenney **Designer:** Lauren Cooper

Library of Congress Cataloging-in-Publication Data

Names: Schwartz, Heather E., author.
Title: Kendrick Lamar : platinum rap artist / Heather E. Schwartz.
Description: Minneapolis : Lerner Publications, 2023. | Series: Gateway biographies | Includes bibliographical references and index. | Audience: Ages 9–14 | Audience: Grades 4–6 | Summary: "Kendrick Lamar has twenty-three tracks and three albums that have sold over a million copies and gone platinum. From childhood to a Grammy-studded career, discover the story of this award-winning rapper"– Provided by publisher.
Identifiers: LCCN 2022057337 (print) | LCCN 2022057338 (ebook) | ISBN 9781728491745 (library binding) | ISBN 9798765602942 (paperback) | ISBN 9781728497549 (ebook)
Subjects: LCSH: Lamar, Kendrick, 1987– —Juvenile literature. | Rap musicians—United States—Biography—Juvenile literature.
Classification: LCC ML3930.L136 S38 2023 (print) | LCC ML3930.L136 (ebook) | DDC 782.421649092 [B]–dc23/eng/20221129

LC record available at https://lccn.loc.gov/2022057337
LC ebook record available at https://lccn.loc.gov/2022057338

Manufactured in the United States of America
1-53113-51123-3/8/2023

TABLE OF CONTENTS

COMING UP IN COMPTON	**8**
MAKING A NAME FOR HIMSELF	**14**
LEVELING UP	**17**
BECOMING A ROLE MODEL	**23**
USING HIS PLATFORM	**27**
CONTINUOUSLY CREATING	**31**
LIVING LEGACY	**35**

IMPORTANT DATES	40
SOURCE NOTES	42
SELECTED BIBLIOGRAPHY	45
LEARN MORE	46
INDEX	47

Kendrick Lamar brings energy and emotion to his performances.

The crowd screamed as words appeared on the large black screen at the back of the stage. "There was an energy in 2011 that formed around the culture of LA," they read. "Rap was back to the basics and the children creating it were birthed from a historic time in history—the Ronald Reagan Era. Sincerely yours, oklama."

The scene went dark. Suspense was building. Everyone in the audience knew why they were there and who they wanted to see next. And then, through a cloud of smoke, the man they'd been waiting for appeared all in white. Dancers wearing matching burgundy suits filled the stage as piano strains filled the air. When Kendrick Lamar launched into the first track from his debut album, *Section.80*, fans rapped along with him. His music's message—that people shouldn't be divided by race—was inspiring and contagious.

Lamar takes the stage on the first day of the 2021 Day N Vegas festival.

Lamar's performance at the Day N Vegas festival in 2021 was his first in two years. But the king of hip-hop never lost his edge. Dedication to his craft transported Lamar from Compton, California, into the global spotlight. He is a true artist whose words speak to people. He represents his culture and even bolstered a movement.

Coming Up in Compton

Kendrick Lamar Duckworth was born on June 17, 1987, in Compton, a city in southern Los Angeles County,

California. From the beginning, he seemed destined for a musical future. His parents, Kenny Duckworth and Paula Oliver, named him after Eddie Kendricks, a founder of the famous musical group The Temptations.

Compton wasn't an easy place to grow up. The city could be dangerous and unpredictable at times. When Kendrick was a preschooler, race riots broke out in the streets. At five he witnessed the murder of a drug dealer near his family's apartment building. But growing up in Compton had its good times too. Kendrick's parents kept him involved in safe, healthy activities. He liked riding his bike and playing basketball. When they had parties, he would sneak out of his room and dance.

Compton, where Kendrick grew up, has a Civic Center Plaza with a sculpture paying tribute to Martin Luther King Jr.

THE LA RIOTS

In 1991 three white Los Angeles police officers viciously beat Rodney King, a Black man. Other officers watched and did nothing. The following year, a jury found the officers not guilty of using too much force. People were outraged by the verdict. Protest riots erupted in LA and became violent.

PEOPLE SET BUILDINGS ON FIRE DURING THE LA RIOTS.

Kendrick was seven when his first sibling was born, and he eventually had two brothers and a sister. When he was eight, rap artists Dr. Dre and Tupac Shakur came to his city to shoot a music video. He watched as they got out of their car to talk to fans. Kendrick never forgot that moment.

Back then his parents called him Man-Man. He acted older than he was and liked to spend time alone watching cartoons and puzzling out how the world worked. He also wanted to know more about how his family made ends meet on a combination of welfare, food assistance, and jobs his mother took styling hair. When he asked his mother, she was happy to talk with him about it. She wanted to help him understand the reality of their lives.

Kendrick had a slight stutter as a child. He was also introverted, and he thrived when expressing himself in writing. He was a good student who especially enjoyed English class. One day he was headed to school and hadn't completed an English homework assignment, so he decided to do it when he got there. He had only ten minutes to write the assignment. Later that day, he learned he'd aced it. While his friends who'd worked harder got Ds and Cs, he got an A.

"From that moment on, I knew I had a gift to actually put words together and draw my own inspirations out on a piece of paper," he said. "That was the beginning when I started writing actual lyrics."

In middle school, Kendrick heard DMX's debut album. He wrote his first lyrics to the music on the album and

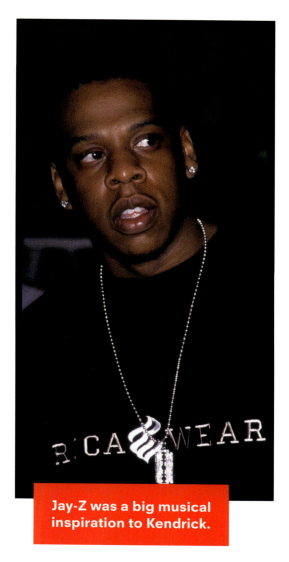

Jay-Z was a big musical inspiration to Kendrick.

never looked back. His early songs drew heavily from DMX and other favorite artists, including Snoop Dogg and Jay-Z. Over time, he started to discover his own voice and his personal style.

Kendrick was also inspired to move forward in music by another role model. His sports hero was basketball player Michael Jordan. He watched Jordan succeed and felt as if his own dreams were in reach. As a young teenager, he felt motivated to reach the same heights of success as his music idols.

In his teens, Kendrick started making some bad choices. He and his friends committed robberies and ran from the police. Sometimes they were unfairly harassed. But Kendrick's parents got strict, and he wanted to change his ways. He had writing as an outlet for the frustrations he felt growing up in a rough neighborhood.

By 2003, when he was sixteen, Kendrick had eleven tracks ready to go. Using the stage name K-Dot, he released his debut mixtape. It was raw hip-hop that combined free verse and strong beats. He distributed it in his neighborhood and worked to get people throughout his home city interested in his music.

Kendrick's efforts paid off in a big way. His mixtape caught the attention of Anthony Tiffith, who ran a new independent record label called Top Dawg Entertainment. Kendrick freestyled for two hours for Tiffith, and he was sold. He signed Kendrick to help him develop his sound and work on an album.

Anthony Tiffith (*left*) signed Kendrick (*right*) to his record label after hearing his rhymes.

Making a Name for Himself

When he was eighteen, Lamar released his second mixtape, *Training Days*, in 2005. The following year, he went on tour with The Game and Jay Rock. He performed for large audiences. It was the first time he'd ever been to a concert. Before that, he never had the money to buy tickets for a show.

Over the next few years, Lamar kept making music. In 2007 he released a mixtape with Jay Rock called *No Sleep Til NYC*. And in 2009, he put out another solo mixtape called *C4*. Up to then, he was performing and creating under the name K-Dot. But by 2010, he felt more confident in the style and sound he was developing. Lamar decided to leave that stage name behind.

Jay Rock was on the Top Dawg label too.

"I was like, 'Y'know what? I want people to know who I am as a person and what I represent,'" he said. "So I woke up one morning and said, the best way to start is to give them me... my name change, my real name."

BLACK HIPPY

As part of Lamar's artistic development, he became part of a hip-hop collective called Black Hippy. Other artists in the group included Ab-Soul, Jay Rock, and ScHoolboy Q. The group never released an album together. But they inspired one another to write and keep working on their music.

Lamar released his fourth solo mixtape, *Overly Dedicated*, in 2010, using his own name but dropping his last name, Duckworth. Tiffith was all for it. He thought Lamar's name sounded like a cologne—and he believed it would help sell albums. So far, they hadn't tried selling any of Lamar's music. It was all available free online. Lamar felt the world should get to know him first. He was more concerned about telling truths in his music than anything. But the pair had a good partnership, with Tiffith offering Lamar a lot of room and time to grow as a creative artist.

In 2011 Lamar had his biggest breakthrough yet. He worked hard on his debut studio album, *Section.80*. It was filled with catchy rhymes and strong messages about issues such as oppression, drug abuse, and growing up under President Ronald Reagan in the 1980s. In April he released the single "HiiiPoWeR" from the *Section.80* album. The title of the song had deep meaning for Lamar. It was about overcoming negativity and maintaining self-respect.

In 2011 Lamar released his first album ever that needed to be bought to be heard.

"The [song's name] represent[s] heart, honor and respect. That's how we carry ourselves in the streets, and just in the world, period," he explained. "[The song] basically is the simplest form of representing just being above all the madness. . . . No matter what the world is going through, you're always going to keep your dignity."

When *Section.80* was released on July 2, Lamar put a price on his music for the first time. In its first week, the album sold about five thousand digital units. It made it onto the *Billboard* 200 chart at No. 113. Lamar's success made him a contender for MTV's Hottest Breakthrough MC award. Though the honor eventually went to Machine Gun Kelly, Lamar was already getting opportunities as a rising star. In November he set off on tour with Drake as an opening act on the Club Paradise Tour.

By 2012 some of the biggest names in the business were talking up the new kid from Compton. Drake, The Game, Snoop Dogg, and Dr. Dre all called Lamar the "New King of the West Coast." In March he signed with Dr. Dre's Aftermath Entertainment. He was ready for a major label and major success.

Leveling Up

When Lamar joined Aftermath Entertainment, he joined a label that already represented big stars such as Eminem and 50 Cent. It looked as though he was on the cusp of reaching major success selling albums. But Lamar's real interest was his music. He aimed to put out his best work, and for his next album he focused on his life, looking back at his upbringing. His songs told a story about the pull of the streets and how his Christian faith and family kept him from following a destructive path. He even used an old photo for the album cover. It showed him as a baby surrounded by family members, and he liked the way it represented the general experience of growing up in Compton.

Lamar quickly joined the ranks of famous rappers such as Dr. Dre, 50 Cent, and Eminem (*left to right*).

In July 2012, Lamar released a single that explored peer pressure and alcohol abuse. When his first major-label album, *good kid, m.A.A.d. city*, came out in October, it was an instant hit. The album soared to No. 2 on the *Billboard* 200 chart.

Once that happened, Lamar was in high demand. He appeared on *Saturday Night Live*, *Late Night with David Letterman*, *Late Night with Jimmy Fallon*, and other shows to promote his album. He'd already built a fan base in the world of hip-hop, but he was leveling up and gaining mainstream fame. Still, he wasn't about to let success go to his head.

"I look in the mirror every day and I'm the same person," he said. "When I walk out in these streets and these people see me as Kendrick Lamar, as a rapper, it's kind of weird to me, cause I'm just a regular person like everybody else."

Lamar performs to promote his album *good kid, m.A.A.d city* in 2012.

Some things about Lamar's life stayed the same. He was religious and stuck by his faith. And he continued dating his high school sweetheart, Whitney Alford, who he called his best friend. Still, compared to most people, Lamar had anything but a normal life. He was constantly touring, on the road with Wiz Khalifa and Mac Miller and headlining the BET Music Matters Tour throughout 2012. And at the end of 2013, he joined Kanye West on the Yeezus Tour.

In 2014 he was nominated for seven Grammy Awards, including Album of the Year and Best New Artist. At the ceremony, he gave his first Grammy performance with Imagine Dragons. The crowd screamed as they delivered a powerful mashup of two of their songs amid flashing lights and clouds of smoke. In the audience, Jay-Z, singer Taylor Swift, Aerosmith lead singer Steven Tyler, and other stars danced and sang along.

When Lamar didn't win any Grammys that year, it was disappointing—not only for him but for fans and even

The crowd went wild when Lamar and Imagine Dragons performed together at the Grammys.

fellow artists he was up against. Hours after winning the award for Best Rap Album, Macklemore posted an image of a text he sent to Lamar. "You got robbed. I wanted you to win. You should have," it said.

But Lamar had other things on his mind. That year he traveled to South Africa to perform several concerts. While there, he saw sights like Robben Island, where activist Nelson Mandela was imprisoned for fighting back against apartheid. The apartheid system in South Africa gave power to white leaders from 1948 to the 1990s. It allowed racial segregation and discrimination against Black South Africans. Lamar was surprised at how moved he was by the experience. The visit expanded his worldview and gave him even more to say in his songs.

"Probably one of the hardest things to do is put [together] a concept on how beautiful a place can be, and tell a person this while they're still in the ghettos of Compton," he said. "I wanted to put that experience in the music."

In 2015 Lamar was nominated for two Grammys, and this time, he won Best Rap Song and Best Rap Performance. By then Lamar was earning a reputation as a different kind of artist. He was thoughtful, ambitious, and focused. While other musical artists indulged in alcohol and cigarettes, he preferred Fruity Pebbles cereal and Lunchables. He aimed to be the best at what he did while inspiring other rappers to up their game and fight back. He thought that kind of competition could make everyone in the industry even better.

Lamar's music flew up the charts while he kept his personal life pretty private.

"If my edge is dull, my sword is dull, and I don't want to fight another guy whose sword is dull," he explained. "If you've got two steel swords going back and forth hitting each other, what's gonna happen? Both of them are going to get sharper."

Becoming a Role Model

By 2015 Lamar was a household name and famous all over the world. But he was still a private person who tried to live a normal life. He had a condo near his old apartment building in Compton. Though he shared a lot of himself with fans, he liked to surround himself with friends and family. And he kept quiet about his relationship with Alford, feeling it would be unfair to put her in the spotlight just because he was famous. But early in the year he let fans in on big news in his personal life. He and his longtime girlfriend were engaged. It was a choice that showed how much he loved her and who he was as a person.

Lamar got engaged to Whitney Alford (*left*), his longtime girlfriend.

"I'm loyal to the soil," Lamar said. "At the end of the day you want to always have real people around you period. I always show respect when respect is being given and people that's been by your side, you supposed to honor that. That's how you stand up."

Around then, he released what would become his biggest album yet. It featured Alford as a background singer, and the subject was his present-day life. The songs were about touring and awards but also addressed bigger issues such as racial injustice, police violence, and his personal experiences leaving Compton and learning to be around many kinds of people. Lamar's goal with the album was to reach kids who lived as he did growing up.

When fans streamed the album more than 9.6 million times within a week, the album broke a Spotify record.

WORKING WITH SWIFT

In 2015 Lamar and Taylor Swift were both in LA and decided to collaborate in the studio. He contributed to her song "Bad Blood" on the album *1989*. He was inspired by her lyrics and felt he and Swift had great chemistry working together as musical artists.

By 2015 Lamar's music was breaking records.

It also hit No. 1 on the *Billboard* chart. Lamar was reaching listeners just as he wanted to. It was a strange feeling to know he was being heard when the music he put out was so personal.

"I have to make it where you truly understand: This is me pouring out my soul on the record," he said. "You're gonna feel it because you too have pain. It might not be like mine, but you're gonna feel it."

Lamar knew his work was getting tons of attention. He even caught the ear of the president of the United States. When asked by *People* magazine what his favorite song of the year was, President Barack Obama named track 11 on Lamar's 2015 album. Lamar was thrilled at the news.

"A lot of times we forget that people in higher places are human. To hear that he liked the same kick drums and the same snares that I like, it just makes him that much more relatable as a person, rather than just a president," Lamar said.

President Barack Obama is a fan of Lamar's music.

Many of his fans were kids, and Lamar knew he was becoming a role model for young people. As an introvert, he felt that responsibility push him out of his comfort zone. He showed up for the kids, knowing how important it was to meet with young fans and be there for them. He was also committed to giving back to help future generations. He donated to after-school programs for students in Compton, including $1.5 million for music and arts departments. Before one $50,000 donation from Lamar, his former high school's music department was short on instruments. With Lamar's help, the music students took a trip to a music festival and got enough new instruments to form string and jazz ensembles. In May the California Senate honored him as the 35th Senate District's Generational Icon.

"Being from the city of Compton and knowing the parks that I played at and neighborhoods, I always thought how great the opportunity would be to give back to my community," Lamar said. "To . . . have these young kids look at me as some type of inspiration is an honor."

Using His Platform

In 2016 Lamar was nominated for eleven Grammys. At the ceremony, he performed songs from his 2015 album, and he gave it his all. Entering in shackles, he started off with a song celebrating Black identity while also making a powerful political statement about racial inequity within the prison system. Throughout his set, he included a newly written verse about the 2012 shooting death of Black teenager Trayvon Martin as well as African drumbeats and rhythms. On the stage, he navigated between prison cells and an enormous bonfire. The audience stood at their seats, riveted by the visuals, the music, and the message.

By the end of the night, Lamar walked away with five Grammys: Best Rap Performance, Best Rap Song, Best Rap/Sung Collaboration, Best Music Video, and Best Rap Album.

At the 2016 Grammys. Lamar's performance honored the late Trayvon Martin.

"First off, all glory to God, that's for sure," he said, accepting his award for Best Rap Album. He went on to thank the most important people in his life: his parents and Alford. And he thanked Top Dawg too for "taking these kids out of the projects, out of Compton, and putting them right here on this stage to be the best they can be. We'll never forget that."

Shortly after the Grammys, in March 2016, Lamar took a creative risk and released eight unfinished demos. He called it *untitled unmastered*, and the surprise album instantly soared to No. 1 on the *Billboard* chart. It showed

SEEKING JUSTICE

In 2012 seventeen-year-old Trayvon Martin, a Black teen, was shot and killed in his father's neighborhood in Florida. The white Hispanic American man who killed him was later found not guilty of the crime. Incidents involving police killings of Black people inspired the Black Lives Matter movement, an effort to end discrimination and bring racial justice to Black people in the US.

A MURAL IN NEW YORK CITY PAYS TRIBUTE TO TRAYVON MARTIN.

In 2016 Lamar won a Grammy for his album.

Lamar's talent and star power. Fans were ready to soak in all the beats, rhythms, raps, and messages he had to offer.

Throughout the year, he packed the March Madness Music Festival in Houston and made a surprise appearance onstage with SZA at the Coachella Valley Music and Arts Festival in Indio, California. He headlined at the Essence Festival in New Orleans and at the Global Citizen Festival in New York City. Lamar was committed to his craft and to sharing his music, and his hard work was recognized again with two Grammy nominations in 2017.

He was proud of his success and awards, but not just for himself. Lamar knew he was representing the entire hip-hop community. He aimed to advance the culture, and clearly, his music was having a big effect. One of his songs was even a major part of the Black Lives Matter movement. People sang the song at protests, and it gave them a sense of hope.

Now a superstar, Lamar played at the Coachella Valley Music Festival with SZA in 2016.

"This album did what I wanted it to do," Lamar said of his 2015 album at the end of the year. "That's not necessarily to sell tons of records—though it didn't do bad at that either—but to actually have an impact on the people and on the culture of music."

Continuously Creating

After his 2015 album was released, Lamar didn't miss a beat. "I'm just writing, writing, writing. I keep these tablets on me until I'm inspired to go back in and make the music. I never take a break from my pen, because I pride myself on that," he said.

Sometimes completing a song took a long time, even more than a year. But he always kept working, drawing from ideas in his head, finding the right sounds to fit, and creating sounds of his own. By the time he got to the studio, he was thinking about listeners too and how he could get others to understand his ideas. He always wanted to make real connections with people.

In March 2017, he released a new single. Soon after, in April, Lamar's fourth studio album came out. It included collaborations with singer Rihanna and the band U2. And

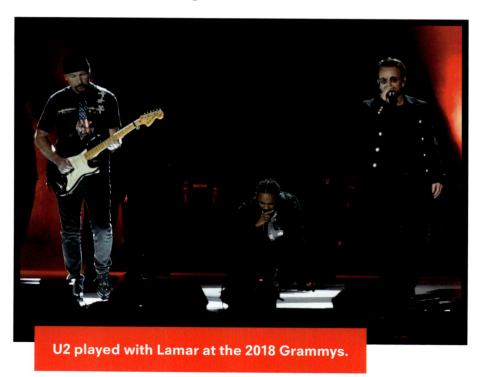

U2 played with Lamar at the 2018 Grammys.

it was much more than a collection of tracks. Lamar had more stories to tell, and this was his way to tell them.

Lamar earned more than a million dollars at each stop on his 2017–2018 tour. But he never forgot where he came from. While his estimated net worth was $30 million, he was careful not to spend lavishly. When he used his money, he did so thoughtfully with a goal of helping others around him. He employed childhood friends; invested; and donated to his former school district, the Red Cross, Habitat for Humanity, and other causes he cared about.

He also never stopped working. In 2018 he produced and curated the soundtrack for the movie *Black Panther* with his friend Anthony Tiffith, from Top Dawg. Meanwhile, his 2017 album was making a big impression. Like his 2015 album, it reached No. 1 on the *Billboard* chart. In 2018 Lamar won Grammys for Best Rap Album for his 2017 album as well as Best Rap Song, Best Rap Performance, Best Music Video, and Best Rap/Sung Performance.

But when his 2017 album won a Pulitzer Prize in April 2018, Lamar became the first rap artist ever to earn this honor. Many people in the music world felt the moment was long overdue. As for Lamar, he was honored and moved to be recognized.

"It's all pieces of me. My musicality has been driving me since I was four years old," Lamar said. "It's just pieces of me, man, and how I execute it is the ultimate challenge."

Lamar accepts the Pulitzer Prize for music in 2018, the first for a hip-hop artist.

By the end of the year, the tour he'd begun in 2017 was over. Lamar was still working on music, but he said he wasn't building up to a new album anytime soon. He wanted to stay connected to his Compton roots even while the world recognized him as hip-hop royalty. Lamar also had a home life away from the spotlight. In July 2019, he and Alford had a daughter.

Lamar had many priorities, and performing was one of them. Throughout 2019 he headlined at Lollapalooza festivals in Chile, Argentina, and Brazil and at a new festival, Day N Vegas, in Las Vegas. In December he closed out the year back in Compton, spending time with neighborhood kids and playing basketball with them at a toy giveaway. True to his values and roots, he dressed down for the event, hanging out in a white T-shirt, black jacket, and black knit hat. On the stage he was larger than life, but in his home city, he knew how to blend in and be the same person he always was.

Living Legacy

In January 2020, rumors spread that Lamar was close to releasing a new album. Soon after, COVID-19 swept through the US and a worldwide pandemic shut down businesses, schools, concerts, and other forms of entertainment. For a long time, life as everyone knew it stopped. Like other people, Lamar pulled back to focus on his family. He also worked on his music. He didn't open up to fans about that period until he wrote about it on his website in August 2021.

"I spend most of my days with fleeting thoughts. Writing. Listening. And collecting old Beach [cruiser bikes]," he wrote. "The morning rides keep me on a hill of silence. I go months without a phone. Love, loss, and grief have disturbed my comfort zone, but the glimmers of God speak through my music and family. While the world around me evolves, I reflect on what matters the most. The life in which my words will land next."

UNIVERSAL STRUGGLES

The year 2020 was difficult for people all over the world. In the US, more than 350,000 died from COVID-19. The country also suffered in other ways. In May police officers in Minneapolis, Minnesota, murdered George Floyd, a Black man, sparking Black Lives Matter protests. More protests followed after President Donald Trump lost the election in November.

Many fans hoped that his note implied a new album was coming soon. They expected his new music would reflect the difficult times of the past year.

When Lamar appeared onstage at the Day N Vegas festival in November 2021, it was the first time he'd been on a stage since 2019. He opened with songs from *Section.80* and moved on to feature music from other albums. Fans were ecstatic to have him back. And Lamar was happy to be there.

By early 2022, three of Lamar's albums and twenty-three of his songs had sold more than a million copies. He was recognized by the Recording Industry Association of America as a certified platinum artist.

He was scheduled to perform at the Super Bowl halftime show. Dr. Dre was also set to perform. There were reports that the NFL wanted to censor parts of the artists' performance.

As the day of the showdown between the Los Angeles Rams and the Cincinnati Bengals drew closer, people were excited that the Super Bowl was showcasing hip-hop. But some said the NFL should show more support for Black culture and communities.

On February 13, the halftime show kicked off with Dr. Dre behind a mock music mixing board. He and Snoop Dogg performed together. Mary J. Blige belted out a solo song. Eminem added a hit of his own, taking a knee in the end, a gesture some professional athletes have used during the national anthem at games to protest racial injustice. Lamar brought his work to the mix,

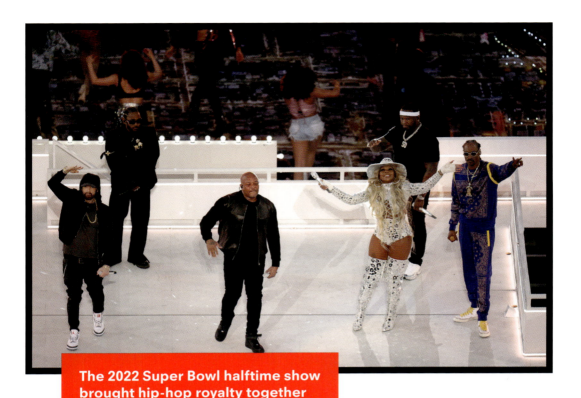

The 2022 Super Bowl halftime show brought hip-hop royalty together for a memorable performance.

leaving out a controversial lyric about the police. Some said he was censored. Others believed he made the choice on his own. Still, when hip-hop took center stage at the Super Bowl halftime show, a long overdue milestone was achieved. More than one hundred million people tuned in to watch.

Just a few months later, in May 2022, Lamar finally dropped his long-awaited fifth studio album, a double album with eighteen tracks. Throughout *Mr. Morale & the Big Steppers*, he tackled modern themes, rapping about capitalism, COVID-19, faith, and his own role as a voice

A NEW NICKNAME

By 2022 Lamar was calling himself oklama. He didn't explain what it meant. Some theorized that "ok" meant he was doing all right, "la" stood for Los Angeles, and "ma" was a reference to his mother. Others believed he used the name oklama as a reference to President Barack Obama.

for the Black community. Reviewers called it both fun and philosophical. And the album was much more than that. Through his new music, Lamar opened up even more to fans. He used his songs to reveal he was working on personal issues with a therapist. He announced through the cover art that his family had expanded. A snapshot showed he and Alford with their toddler daughter and a new baby.

"It's stuff that I've written that's just now seeing daylight, because I wasn't secure with myself in order to do it," he said of the album. "When I did this, it was kind of the marker and the growth of everything I've always wanted to say. I think that was really my purpose of writing my way out of things that I was feeling, from the time I was 9 years old, all the way up to 35."

Lamar worried about how people might react to things he said about family, relationships, and other topics. Making the decision to put certain songs on the album

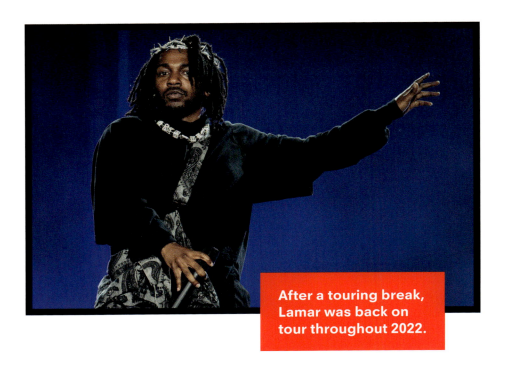

After a touring break, Lamar was back on tour throughout 2022.

was hard. But in the end, he believed his messages could help people—including his children and future grandchildren.

Lamar developed his voice over decades. As he honed his skills and gained confidence, his music spoke personal truths while touching millions of lives. As he worked, he built a legacy that changed culture. There is no doubt he'll have more to say—and contribute—in the future.

IMPORTANT DATES

1987 Kendrick Lamar Duckworth is born June 17 in Compton, California.

2003 At sixteen he joins Top Dawg Entertainment and releases his first mixtape.

2005 At eighteen he releases his second mixtape, *Training Days*.

2007 He releases *No Sleep Til NYC* with Jay Rock.

2009 He releases *C4*.

2010 He releases his fourth solo mixtape, *Overly Dedicated*, using his new artist name.

2011 He releases his debut studio album, *Section.80*.

2012 He signs with Aftermath Entertainment. His first major studio album, *good kid, m.A.A.d. city*, hits No. 2 on the *Billboard* 200 chart.

2015 He becomes engaged to Whitney Alford and releases another album.

2016 He wins five Grammy Awards. He releases *untitled unmastered*.

2017 He releases another album, one of his most highly praised yet.

2018 He wins the first Pulitzer Prize for hip-hop music.

2022 He performs in the Super Bowl halftime show. He releases his fifth album, *Mr. Morale & the Big Steppers*.

2023 He wins a Grammy for *Mr. Morale & the Big Steppers* and a single.

SOURCE NOTES

7 NFR Podcast, Twitter Post, November 13, 2021, 10:01 p.m., https://twitter.com/nfr_podcast/status/1459733317184544772.

11 Andres Tardio, "Here's What Kendrick Lamar's Childhood Was Like," MTV, July 6, 2015, https://www.mtv.com/news/hmvc3x /kendrick-lamar-childhood.

14 Syron, "Kendrick Lamar Talks Name Change, Growing Up in Compton," HardKnockTV, June 10, 2011, https://hiphopdx.com /news/id.15501/title.kendrick-lamar-talks-name-change -growing-up-in-compton.

16 "J. Cole Produced Kendrick Lamar's Debut Single 'HiiiPoWer," DailyRapFacts, accessed January 28, 2023, https://dailyrapfacts .com/12500/j-cole-produced-kendrick-lamars-debut-single -hiiipower/.

17 David Astramskas, "New King of the West Coast—Kendrick Lamar Will Be at 2012 Ballislife HS All-American Game," Ballislife.com, March 16, 2012, https://ballislife.com/new-king -of-the-west-coast-kendrick-lamar-will-be-at-2012-ballislife-hs -all-american-game/.

18 "Kendrick Lamar: Good Kid, M.A.A.D. City Interview," YouTube video, 33:17, posted by Celebrity Interviews, accessed January 28, 2023, https://www.youtube.com/watch?v=54J_gltVvz8.

21 Jon Caramanica, "Finding a Place in the Hip Hop Ecosystem," *New York Times*, January 28, 2014, https://www.nytimes .com/2014/01/28/arts/music/finding-a-place-in-the-hip-hop -ecosystem.html.

21 Rodney Carmichael and Sidney Madden, " 'Black Panther: The Album' Is Kendrick Lamar's Parallel, Pan-African Universe," NPR, February 21, 2018, https://www.npr.org/sections /allsongs/2018/02/21/587334273/black-panther-the-album-is -kendrick-lamar-s-parallel-pan-african-universe.

22 Lizzy Goodman, "Kendrick Lamar: Hip-Hop's Newest Old-School Star," *New York Times Magazine*, June 29, 2014, https://www.nytimes.com/2014/06/29/magazine/kendrick-lamar-hip-hops-newest-old-school-star.html.

24 Aicha FD., "Kendrick Lamar Is Engaged," *XXL*, April 3, 2015, https://www.xxlmag.com/kendrick-lamar-engaged-whitney-alford/.

25 Joe Coscarelli, "Kendrick Lamar on His New Album and the Weight of Clarity," *New York Times*, March 22, 2015, https://www.nytimes.com/2015/03/22/arts/music/kendrick-lamar-on-his-new-album-and-the-weight-of-clarity.html.

25 Joe Coscarelli, "Kendrick Lamar on a Year of Knowing What Matters," *New York Times*, January 3, 2016, https://www.nytimes.com/2016/01/03/arts/music/kendrick-lamar-on-a-year-of-knowing-what-matters.html.

27 Sara Zahedi, "Rapper Kendrick Lamar Uses Music, Money as a Vehicle for Social Change," *Youth Today*, May 28, 2015, https://youthtoday.org/2015/05/rapper-kendrick-lamar-uses-music-money-as-vehicle-for-social-change/.

28 "Watch Kendrick Lamar Win Best Rap Album for 'To Pimp a Butterfly,' GRAMMY Rewind," YouTube video, 2:07, posted by the Recording Academy/GRAMMYs, accessed January 28, 2023, https://www.youtube.com/watch?v=hQbxKYyy42c.

31 Coscarelli, "Year of Knowing What Matters."

31–32 Joe Coscarelli, "Kendrick Lamar on the Grammys, Black Lives Matter and His Big 2015," *New York Times*, December 29, 2015, https://www.nytimes.com/2016/01/03/arts/music/kendrick-lamar-on-a-year-of-knowing-what-matters.html.

33 Andre Gee, "Kendrick Lamar Is Back. How Will His Album Reflect the World's Changes?," Complex, April 18, 2022, https://www.complex.com/music/kendrick-lamar-is-back-world-has-changed/.

35 Jordan Rose, "Kendrick Lamar's Surprise Announcement Has Hip-Hop Fans Going Wild on Twitter," Complex, August 20, 2021, https://www.complex.com/music/kendrick-lamar-suprise-announcement-has-hip-hop-fans-going-wild-on-twitter/.

38 Archie Brydon, "Kendrick Lamar Talks Making *Mr. Morale & the Big Steppers*," whynow, accessed January 28, 2023, https://whynow.co.uk/read/kendrick-lamar-talks-making-mr-morale-the-big-steppers.

SELECTED BIBLIOGRAPHY

Bauer, Patricia. "Kendrick Lamar: American Musician." Britannica. Accessed January 28, 2023. https://www.britannica.com/biography/Kendrick-Lamar.

Caramanica, Jon. "Finding a Place in the Hip Hop Ecosystem." *New York Times*, January 28, 2014. https://www.nytimes.com/2014/01/28/arts/music/finding-a-place-in-the-hip-hop-ecosystem.html.

Coscarelli, Joe. "Kendrick Lamar on His New Album and the Weight of Clarity." *New York Times*, March 22, 2015. https://www.nytimes.com/2015/03/22/arts/music/kendrick-lamar-on-his-new-album-and-the-weight-of-clarity.html.

——. "Kendrick Lamar on a Year of Knowing What Matters." *New York Times*, January 3, 2016. https://www.nytimes.com/2016/01/03/arts/music/kendrick-lamar-on-a-year-of-knowing-what-matters.html.

Eels, Josh. "The Trials of Kendrick Lamar." *Rolling Stone*, June 22, 2015. https://www.rollingstone.com/music/music-news/the-trials-of-kendrick-lamar-33057/.

Gee, Andre. "Kendrick Lamar Is Back. How Will His Album Reflect the World's Changes?" Complex, April 18, 2022. https://www.complex.com/music/kendrick-lamar-is-back-world-has-changed/.

Goodman, Lizzy. "Kendrick Lamar: Hip-Hop's Newest Old-School Star." *New York Times Magazine*, June 29, 2014. https://www.nytimes.com/2014/06/29/magazine/kendrick-lamar-hip-hops-newest-old-school-star.html.

Tardio, Andres. "Here's What Kendrick Lamar's Childhood Was Like." MTV, July 6, 2015. https://www.mtv.com/news/hmvc3x/kendrick-lamar-childhood.

Zahedi, Sara. "Rapper Kendrick Lamar Uses Music, Money as a Vehicle for Social Change." *Youth Today*, May 28, 2015. https://youthtoday.org/2015/05/rapper-kendrick-lamar-uses-music-money-as-vehicle-for-social-change/.

LEARN MORE

Britannica Kids: Rap
https://kids.britannica.com/kids/article/rap/353697

Crawford, Terrance. *Bust Your Own Rhymes . . . and Discover the Star You Are!* New York: Scholastic, 2022.

Grammy Awards: Kendrick Lamar
https://www.grammy.com/artists/kendrick-lamar/17949

Shea, Therese M. *Kendrick Lamar: Becoming the Voice of Compton.* New York: Enslow, 2020.

Wilson, Lakita. *Lizzo: Breakout Artist.* Minneapolis: Lerner Publications, 2021.

INDEX

Aftermath Entertainment, 17
Alford, Whitney, 19, 23–24, 34, 38

Black Hippy, 15
Black Lives Matter, 29–30, 35

Compton, CA, 8–9, 17, 21, 23–24,
    26–28, 34
COVID-19, 35, 37

Day N Vegas, 8, 34, 36
Duckworth, Kenny, 9

Floyd, George, 35

good kid, m.A.A.d. city, 18
Grammy Awards, 20–21, 27–28, 30,
    33

Kendricks, Eddie, 9
King, Rodney, 10

Martin, Trayvon, 27, 29
mixtapes, 13–15
Mr. Morale & the Big Steppers, 37

No Sleep Til NYC, 14

Obama, Barack, 25, 38
Oliver, Paula, 9
Overly Dedicated, 15

Pulitzer Prize, 33

Section.80, 7, 15–16, 36
stage names and nicknames, 7, 11,
    13–14, 38
Super Bowl, 36–37

35th Senate District's Generational
    Icon, 27
Tiffith, Anthony, 13, 15, 33
Top Dawg Entertainment, 13, 28, 33
Training Days, 14

untitled unmastered, 28

PHOTO ACKNOWLEDGMENTS

Image credits: Theo Wargo/WireImage/Getty Images, p. 2; Allen J. Schaben/ Los Angeles Times/Getty Images, pp. 6, 8; Underawesternsky/Shutterstock, p. 9; David Butow/Corbis/Getty Images, p. 10; Ron Galella, Ltd./Ron Galella Collection/Getty Images, p. 12; Noel Vasquez/GC Images/Getty Images, p. 13; Frank Schwichtenberg/Wikipedia Commons, p. 14; AP Photo/Matt Sayles, p. 16; Presley Ann/Getty Images, p. 18; Tim Mosenfelder/Getty Images, p. 19; Robert Gauthier/Los Angeles Times/Getty Images, p. 20; AP Photo/Chris Pizzello/Invision, p. 22; Johnny Nunez/Getty Images, p. 23; Scott Dudelson/ Getty Images, p. 25; MANDEL NGAN/AFP/Getty Images, p. 26; Kevin Winter/ WireImage/Getty Images, pp. 28, 30; Ben Gabbe/Getty Images, p. 29; Emma McIntyre/Getty Images, p. 31; Kevin Winter/Getty Images, p. 32; AP Photo/ Bebeto Matthews, p. 34; Gregory Shamus/Getty Images, p. 37; Jason Koerner/ Getty Images, p. 39.

Cover: AP Photo/Chris Pizzello/Invision.